From a Cliff

ANDY BROWN
From a Cliff

2002

Published by Arc Publications
Nanholme Mill, Shaw Wood Road
Todmorden, Lancs. OL14 6DA

Copyright © Andy Brown 2002

Design by Tony Ward
Printed at Antony Rowe Limited
Eastbourne, East Sussex

ISBN 1 900072 31 9

Most of these poems have been previously published.
Thanks are due to the editors of the following
magazines, and web-magazines, where they first
appeared:
Acumen, Fire, Flying Post, Kunapipi, New Writing 10
(edited by George Szirtes and Penelope Lively), *Oasis,
Orbis, Osiris, Poetry etc, Poetry Quarterly Review, Salt,
Slope, Stand, Tremblestone* and to the editor of *Voices
for Kosovo* (Stride, 1999). Two poems were first
published in the pamphlet *The Sleep Switch* (Odyssey
Poets, 1996). Several poems were first published in a
collaborative publication with David Morley, *Of
Science* (The Worple Press, 2001). *Devon Apples* was
originally published as a chapbook by Maquette
(1999).

With special thanks to David Morley.

The publishers acknowledge financial assistance from
Yorkshire Arts Board.

CONTENTS

LAND

The Thread / 9
'What We Think of as Home…' / 10
The Water Cycle / 11
City Bus Ride / 12
Stes-Maries-de-la-Mer / 13
Finding Home / 14
Shakkei / 15
A Poem of Gifts / 19

SEA

Cavatina / 23
A Lifting Wreck / 24
From a Cliff / 25
Spawning Grounds / 26
On the Bluff / 27
Walking a Beach, Any Beach / 28
Two Miniatures / 29
Vertigo / 30
Some Kind of Sea Light / 31
Across the Waves / 32

SHIFTING TIDES

The Matter Rests / 37
How We Give / 38
The Sleep Switch / 39
How Old is the Light? / 41
The Broken Mould / 42
Chess Moves / 43
Lecture on the Theory of Being No. 33 / 44
An Old Cartoon / 45
Landscape with Mountains / 46
No Reason / 47
Fragments for an Indeterminate Friend / 48
Photo in a Mirror of a Woman Descending Stairs / 51
Devon Apples / 53

Notes / 56

This collection is dedicated to
Molly May
my land, sea & shifting tide – my daughter

LAND

This is the earth we dream and childishly colour.

Don De Lilo, *The Names*

THE THREAD

Long before we see the swallows find their way
back home, we sense their coming in our blood,
something unnameable, like the sound of the
breathing we come to recognise as our own,
or the strange shrieks of foxes on lake margins,
which remind us that it is, perhaps, intangible
geometries that tie all this together, or how

sometimes at night, we think we hear timber
falling in a forest we cannot name, a wooded
col on the peak of our loves & find ourselves
blessed by the presence of animals & trees,
a calligraphy of light high in their branches & there,
in a crevice, we find the thread that binds us to others –
the knowledge that all we have to do is change.

'WHAT WE THINK OF AS HOME'
after John Burnside

I lived for more than twenty years
with my husband & sons
in Jiangsu Province,

the black terrace under
the white magnolias;
the arcane laws of feng shui.

Now I sit between morello trees,
suffused in the past
& the vanished.

Pausing at the rotting windows
there is the familiar. Time
still forms the tasks that keep me here.

Nowhere else do I feel I belong
as I do here. Dawn is still an hour
away. These winter nights linger & linger.

THE WATER CYCLE
for Sally Meyer

> 'Think of how language would be
> if all there was to read were headstones.'

Framed by fences & telegraph lines
as in Spencer's Resurrection painting
the mourners trudge uphill until a
Church of Scotland roadsign jerks them
left beneath the Yes Yes on the gas tank.

The coffin's borne by hand into the open
autumn air, upon a stripped pine door
with stretcher handles. Stooped & beret'd
men march on ahead, the women drag their
30's shoes behind. Gulls trace mental lines

above the lichen-covered roofs. Seafood
enters port in freezer skips – these graveyards
always sited where the sea & shoreline fuse.
A skein of cloud the length of the horizon
divides the sky & sea, mirroring each other;

what the other would be. The estuary broadens,
the current slows, as life on shore resumes
its common pace. This is all there is then –
one brief crawl up the world's edge; a glimpse of
impossible light. 'Outside the wind blew.'

CITY BUS RIDE

'I have need to busy my heart with quietude.'
　　　　　– *Rupert Brooke*, The Busy Heart

It is morning in the city. I have boarded a bus,
not knowing where the driver's to, or the route
she will take. Whenever I am able to escape my
self, I ride for hours like this on roads around
the city's parks, with their tall trees filtering sun
light & their inviting rugs of grass. When the
bus leaves, she goes from outside a coffee-house
where men smoke, drink strong coffee & play
dominoes, even at this hour. The city is vibrant
with motion's music. Desires head in all directions.
Ribbons of roads fan out from the heart & make
the city throb with rhythms of legend & myth –
there is something ancient in her, like the presence
of the ziggurat of Ur.
　　　　　　　　　　At the end of a bridge,
where the buildings stand in disrepair, the ritual
of two people shaking hands, cryptically symbolic.
A third man on his knees holds congregation with
a flock of birds. Children brush past him on their
hurried way to school, bubbling into the distance
like beads of amber or faience in an ancient trader's
hands. 'Buzzing with life,' the girl beside me says,
although it's never life itself we see; it's the woman
& woman alone we see moving, as she walks
between high terraces banked with plants; the flex
in her arms & legs, the torsion in her back. It is
the experience of our world that makes it real
& nothing more. All philosophy teaches that.

STES-MARIES-DE-LA-MER

'Les Chevaliers?' you said & we made it in time
to see five riders pass on horseback – those
fabled, snow-white creatures that metamorphose
as they grow, born brown, or black & blanched pure white
by four years old – crossing the quiet inlet of the delta,
serene in the shadow of juniper trees. Later,
in the cool church, we touched the disused props
of the lame who came to walk; the patches
of the blind who came to see in this haven
of miracles & changes, where the bones of Saints
are carried through the streets each May,
down to the sea in a healing cavalcade

& later still we also rode those changelings,
our stallions standing firm at first, though throwing
back their heads – the air resonant with insects –
& then, sensing something inexperienced
in the way we held the reigns, bolting through
the shallow lagoons in an explosion of hooves,
our muscles & theirs screaming with the violent flash
of summer, until they dropped us, their muzzles
foaming in sweat & we slumped from our saddles,
shocked & fighting for breath in the chafing grass.

FINDING HOME

What remains is not so much the thrill
of walking down a dark road to the still
of night, where days ferment & the moon
sucks out the juices of the restless dream;
nor is it the narrow way reminding
us that what we can't bring back gnaws
at regret; it is instead the certainty that doing
nothing is a tedious process. It is easy to be sure
of the sudden, yet not so simple to picture the slow
accretions of time in Sumer, Babylon & Ur.

Everyone, they say, eventually finds their home:
a ghetto house of zinc; a plot of wood & water;
the summit of lazy talk in the village square.
The journey's only part of it, what's hard is being there.

SHAKKEI
Japanese: 'borrowed scenery'

1. SHAKKEI

A woman frees some captured birds.
She is later rescued from a riverbed
by swallows that carry her back to earth.

The light moves north.
Dawn draws across the horizon –
a saturated woman walks back into history.

Shaping the site, she places herself
in the landscape, fleshing it out in the mind –
a dense stand of maple,

each branch the idea of a sacred grove
near a stream where birds drink.
There are only two seasons: Desire & Return.

2. WINTERING UNDERWATER

'Swallows winter underwater.'
– *The Archbishop of Uppsala,* 1555

Beginning to end has begun.
Now streams & deep marshes
sustain migratory breaths

fluctuating seasonally. The river
has reached a dénouement – this
daily up & down stuff.

How do they know when
it's time to go & sleep where
water laps? The map says

where they are; the compass
the direction. Here swallows
gather & meanings grow,

the banks in patterns of flux,
learning the waters & waiting
in rivers 'til Spring. On the surface,

shadows of willow trees dance
to celebrate remembered ground.
Deep down, the swallows sleep.

3. SHE TURNED INTO THE RIVER

She turned into the river
as a cloud turns into rain,
her last few moments spread

across the wide alluvial plain,
like the leaves of windswept
willows on the river's edge...

bud-burst to mouse ear,
mouse ear to full blade,
late blossom petal fall.

4. A BODY OF WATER

A body of water,
of rivers & lakes,
lying in the geographic heart.

The bank trees turning,
each oak & hazel etched
against an evening sky,

their central roots
that find deep levels,
expanding over meadows

& monopolizing streams.
Life has changed
the supporting land:

one moment I stood
at the river's edge; the next
I was swept away,

like letters chalked
on the hull of a boat
stuck on the estuary flats.

5. THE AIR IS FULL OF MOUNTAINS

The air is full of mountains,
screaming clouds – an orange mist
that sings as a Kabuki actor sings.

Passing over the lip, the air recites
the different names of plants
& birds – willows, swallows –

naming the land on which I stand…
names, names falling on the head
as so much rain falls.

A POEM OF GIFTS

I want to give thanks for the garden
   already in bloom this March
   as I sit here with you, curled
   like an aleph in your papoose;
for the balsam of your chatter,
   echoic & fluid,
   like an elver in the wash;
for the flexion of your tongue
   throwing muscular vowels
   into the fuzz of sun & dew,
   like the musical chimes of a gamelan;
for the brouhaha of the blackbird
   as it picks at a red berry,
   or last winter's lingering
   hips & haws;
for the synod of starlings
   gathered in the oak;
for the peony's growth
   we can almost hear
   surging through the soil;
for my dibber pushing through the clod,
   to sow the seed that promises blue
   borage at the bottom of the plot;
for the bubble of the acorn
   exploding underground;
for the dewlaps on cattle
   chewing cud in the fields beyond,
   their calves impatient
   at their udders;
for the kazoo of insects
   busy at the nectaries
   of cowslips & daffodils;
for the fresco of morning;
for the whole gamut & hex of spring;
for your mother
   in her workshop,
   unloading the kiln;
for the hubbub & jabber

of her radio;
for the hoop of love
　　that rolls on
　　with no beginning & no end;
for the unknowable nuances
　　of change;
for the nub of pleasures which elude me;
for the koan of '*Why?*'
for the ingots of your eyes;
for the honey of your dribble;
for your *tabula rasa*.

SEA

– God! he said quietly. Isn't the sea what Algy
calls it: a great sweet mother? The snotgreen sea.
The scrotumtightening sea.

James Joyce, *Ulysses*

CAVATINA

Yesterday unfolds tomorrow with today's hands
draining into the blue – a shifting land
where feeling most at home approaches
stillness. Evaporating mildly in the shallows,
or drifting like fine snow, I am just a visitor.
Beach deposits crumble under brilliant stars –
a montage of blocks along the barren strip,
feigning death like stranded fish.

A second coastline starts beyond the first;
this frozen sea of light at the sound's edge.
One thing is clear, the moment won't last long
high on the shore: night after night it comes,
approaching the land as though it's ablaze,
cruising narrow cliffs under waning moons,
revealing life stories baked to sinews in the high
strand's wake, like driftwood cast along the littoral.

Bells ring for a second time this evening
marking some significance or, simply,
to remind between the peals that we are called to
things – whatever things might be – as if to ask me
Who I am? What I am? Where I'm going ?
We know who we are. We are who we are
the day we are born, spend the rest of our lives
becoming someone else, like rocks in rising tides.

A LIFTING WRECK

She came off the rocks at night, by remote
islands in a coastal bay – black as far as
I could see – the zooplankton blooming
in luminescent drifts & pods of whales,
more accurate than maps, following their
prey. Some seabirds ascended & others
descended... it didn't matter which way
they were going, as long as they were going.

She'd gone. The beach was silent. Starfish
& anemones moved quietly in their cracks.
I talked to Disbelief & found it was
a perfectly level mirror – the false
impression that the endless well of lights
continues & never goes out; the moon
reaching into the moment & blinding
the dark with its everyday-ness.

Looking out along her northbound trail,
the question just became a question of
where I thought I was. That much I knew,
but would I ever get to leave? The tips of our
shadows were vanishing points, like trails of
moonlight, somewhere outside of the moment.
After years of believing this boat would float,
the error was it didn't ever matter.

FROM A CLIFF
for George Szirtes

Say we find ourselves sitting with our feet
over the edge of a cliff, the horizon bending
not only ahead but all around & even inwards,
pregnant in its curvature – this grassy ledge
we call a home, the illusion of an island –
what of the idea we are then; the image conveyed?
Here are our opening arms, high above the truth of it.

As pigeons in a city park begin the day
& test the sky, subsiding into flurried clusters,
we sit as we are, not doing what we are
supposed to be thinking, lifeless in suspension
& what of keeping a notebook of the days
we've made up in our mind? Is that all
this is all about – recorded time?

'An idea is nothing but the start of tears;
the flutter of fear beneath the skin,'
our fingers whisper & that rings true,
not only because ideas become confused,
but also because of speech itself becoming
a part of the pain – speaking of jumping
to swim in the ache of the opening air.

Today spills southward using light as a lure,
drifting in to air's anticipation. Inside
its gates again, voices – the living words
our hearts pick up, all dying of darkness.
We sit abutting change & yes it's true, almost
to the point of smiling, we learn loneliness,
with solely a monopoly of spirit to reassure its limits.

SPAWNING GROUNDS

For nights & nights we sail the seasons,
anchoring off the submerged islands'
grey & inimical cliffs. Here the talk
is of what is – water, air & rock –
coves in cobalt, bights, blue waves,
the bay with its jetty & debris.

This is where ideas spawn, migrating
to sea where they fatten & mature
only to return & die soon after
in shallow sections of the sound;
these spawning seas a common ground
that run us ashore as we're speaking.

ON THE BLUFF

Deeply inscribed with names, the landscape
starts talking, much as mountains & rivers
emit sounds: the drowsy hum of wind,
the mesmerizing blue patois of water.
We pick our way through the heavy drift,
like birds in flight burdened with prey.
On the bluff beyond the beach,
the water & land appear the same thing:
spots for exploration; whales spouting
ahead of us; a pale light blurring two worlds
in a tone of forgiveness, like two hands linked,
aware of each other long before contact is made,
just as along the battered coastline quiet returns
to the cathedral stacks of rocks that lie obscured
some distance from the shore, massive shapes
that watch the changes in light, as suddenly
darkness is here, missing the point it turned –
presuming that there is a point it turned –
these memories of ocean-going ships, their lines
of windows shuttered up & anchored in their history.

WALKING A BEACH, ANY BEACH

1.
The sun hugs the sear shore. We walk the sand
& talk it through.   Light spills across the day,
changing your face, hidden behind its veil of words,

like a breeze that hangs too long above the cliffs
& loses its freshness, unaware a great love has
descended.   Children hunt for crabs below low tide.

What anchors them here, when something
as slight as a wind-shift knocks us over,
or the constant tidal tugging drags us out to sea?

2.
Our conversation turns to birds
& flies off into the sunset.
Nesting terns pay it no mind at all,

but we, we are overwhelmed
by the flight of our words, warm
in the grace of these minutes we share.

3.
Slipping down dunes to the water below,
tongues of land loll out beyond the sterile hills.
The estuary lies in a profound darkness
that blooms so suddenly & effusively.

Bones of shipwrecks fleck the pastures
of shore, like clouds of seabirds waiting
for some oceanic wind to pick them up
in a shaft of interior light, working the thermals

like thoughts, high above the slip-face of
cascading sand; the incognito gestures of the sea.

TWO MINIATURES

1.
We write our presence on the shore with feet
& wander to the point by calling names
through the spray. Life moves at the pace
of paddling. Your steps echo mine.

The wind draws tears from the corners
of my eyes, as relics of our origins at sea.
The whole day feels like my birthday;
not so much as presents, but the gift –

'Thank god for you; thank god I'm still alive.'

2.
She broke up, died & scattered
like a spray of sparks rising

with a great flame. I saw in her
an echo-chamber of the spirit.

Giants stood aside to let her pass.
She was so beautifully faulted;

a cliff undercut with crystal caves.

VERTIGO
i.m. J.H.

The curved horizon stares so silently,
inviting you to your ancestral shore –
a ship set loose on seas of memory.

A bird beginning flight – you pick up speed.
Above, the terns that saw young Icarus fall.
The curved horizon stares so silently.

A voice within the rock demands you leap.
Suddenly you're heavenrushing; through the door –
a ship set loose on seas of memory.

The names of those who leave us rest in peace,
as dust settles on the catafalque.
The curved horizon stares so silently.

Disappearance holds a thread of mystery.
You jump the nest & fly, begin to fall –
a ship set loose on seas of memory.

I look down at the slip face & roiling sea.
As if arranged, the breakers part & roar.
The curved horizon stares so silently
at ships set loose on seas of memory.

SOME KIND OF SEA LIGHT

'The root of all things is green,'
says the Arab philosopher Haly.

Pollen analysis proves it. Even
in the night the green comes over.

At midsummer, the vernal equinox,
only one wavelength is visible.

But what of the colours we know
as love; the urge to fall asleep

inside the carapace?   Stepping close,
the light cuts understanding.

Our skins condense dismay.
We face each other wordlessly

papering over the cracks the way
we use words to paper over

the joins between things – not that
things are joined but held apart;

not even that there are things themselves
(if the Buddha's to be believed),

only the ideas of things, which brings
us back to words themselves, the way

they oscillate like the movements of
a child's puzzle, shifting tiles one by one

until a pattern is formed – ships
in a sudden & luminous calm.

You know, I like boats.   I see
sea-green & it's the deep I want.

ACROSS THE WAVES

'We rise at five & haul our brains out til eleven'
– a large fish sees it reflecting the light & strikes –
& anchored there   deep in the flesh   the water's edge.
Beaches slip from underneath these trackless regions.
Their wake is completed by our heads jutting just above
the bow. Bystanders ooh & aah at these cathedrals
& realise Jesus chose five fishermen to join him.
Even when we're gone we'll choose such excuses
to cross the bay on cracking ice & the desert
in our waterless eyes will still be chiselled at –
a special efflorescence of civilisation.

~

Nature has composed a masterpiece of bathos;
a collective groan across the ages.
Its craft professes to uncover much
like the overturned hull of a working boat at low tide.
It's a good sized craft   some kind of utility vessel.
I can tell you how it was built
how it was steered & how repairs were made
but as soon as we excavate something
we assure its destruction – the boat itself will crumple into pieces.

~

Other fragments of lost lives have emerged along the beach.
Along this coast Circe revealed to Ulysses the way to Hades.
We could descend those steps onto the tongue of land
where waves lap under windows as we bathe
but the unanswered questions are burrowing everywhere.
We   who are just on the wrong side of the sound
the continuous vibration & harmonic tremor
launch the inflatables
but within fifteen minutes of the call to action
we are falling backwards.

How did the waves begin?
Could it have been the helmsman?
Was the boat already under sail?
Or was it that in the aquarium all we had seen was a blur
whereas here   to our astonishment   things
popped out of the water like bouncing raindrops
while we paraded our relic blood across the waves?

~

Circe's thumb of land becomes as a big ballerina.
Water flows over her uninterrupted like a band –
a low monotonous chant that belonged to her father.
Choirs of palms   pearl curtain of cloud
& sea hanging off-shore. The sea is blue;
we shine wet & red. The captain smiles.
Within the wrinkles   the early light of morning
breathing deep in mammoth swells
briny   but not too sharp
sweet   but not too much so.
The sea is *yes*.

SHIFTING TIDES

… Then we,
As we beheld her striding there alone,
Knew that there never was a world for her
Except the one she sang and, singing, made.

Wallace Stevens, *The Idea of Order at Key West*

THE MATTER RESTS

There's an old Chinese saying: Before one dies,
one tells the truth. Okay, but when? That calls
for a beer. When I think of it, it begins innocently
enough: the clear air; the stone steps leading up to
the old city, glittering in the low-hung sun; our daily
lives getting on with it in the pre-dawn stillness,
but then Things & Words get in the way, emerging
from the air as if from nowhere, the way the past
rises up to greet us through layers of mud – potsherds,
bones, fragments of text – part of the inscrutable
landscape which holds the surprises that fill
our lives. Not that anyone is paying much attention;
it is years before we see what we have – the small clues
that lead on to this twilight, which seems to last forever

HOW WE GIVE

Being is always about to begin,
cloaked in the light of our dying,

yet lie quite still & it all blows by,
complex, lodged in how we give,

until we find we need our lives
to find out what we came for:

tides of shifting black that tug us
back to where the puzzling I is rare,

as though we were invisible operators,
dreaming; simply sleeping with the lights on.

THE SLEEP SWITCH

> 'Por los minutos que preceden al sueño...'
> 'For the minutes which precede sleep...'
> — *Borges*

To call them by their real names admits imagination
& intuits the thinking of animals or strangers
speaking the sounds of the answers we seek.
Yet what is so unstable & uncertain as the words
  everyone knows?
All things forgetfulness lifts up hang perishable tomorrow –
knowing that time could polish them, writing it all –
abandoned to the rigours of marasmus & escaping
reason, obstinate in the face of memory.

But it is soon blunted, this spell of blindness,
by reciting the signs in sleep. Rotation & mixing
return the words to astonished palates
& allow us to unburden ourselves,
though we know with faith's mysterious certitude
that nobody dreams it in words, in gilded capitals
& they may remain apocryphal.
Fakirs & yogis with their breathing exercises;
trucks that carry frozen meat,
they each remind us the number of chosen is fixed
& where a harvest of silence & darkness
puts an end to this priceless confusion –
to religious ceremonies & devices up our sleeves –
the misfortune of losing faith obscures the need
to lose the soul to save it,
leaving the refuge abandoned by maddening dawn,
& rediscovers the path that leads from the other side of the face.

All this keeps its hold over the public.
Having come down to the present
we look forward to the models, the opening words
& anomalies that take the form of words,
saying nothing of whole lives in which not a single one
figures. To think it was we who invented those names;

that out there in the world nothing is happening.
To think that the mind would fall into the error of believing
the masses of humanity who swarm around it
today bewildered, yesterday forgotten & tomorrow
        unpredictable
is the understood thing sleeping in the pardonable confusion.

HOW OLD IS THE LIGHT?

Before we can discuss eternity
gravity lengthens the day. Imagine
the limitless space; a football high
in the air above the players' heads;

the so-called paradox of infinity.
You could almost quote the Biblical
statement 'Nothing can be said'
& prove it in the open field of days.

All you have to do is correct the
amounts of light. One assumes
& why not? It's only logical to
assume it's logical to think

although we know this can't be true –
the earth is made up. The key
to understanding the complex lies
in singling out the stars by eye.

Come close to the sun, face to face
with its processes. Look at what
goes on in dying, ask 'How does
a dead star look; how old is the light?'

41

THE BROKEN MOULD

1.
The broken mould conforms in its own way
like the streets & piazzas of a great
metropolis buzzing with shock waves by day
& yet when all subsides little more remains
than the dream of tomorrow's wage
& the debt we owe the past but only pay
by packing up our things & going away.

2.
As the sun's white disk begins to fade
we walk to the twisting beat of waves.
On the top of a cliff by the wind's grace
we watch two boys skimming stones all the way
out to the groynes. Their pebbles seem to say:
'We know exactly where the spray
will rise where next we land.' We stop & pray.

3.
God – we have one chance in two. Those may
seem good odds but they can change
for no one wants to live inside *His* shade.
What we seek devotedly in the failing
light begins to wear away. We fish all day
with little luck; play conspiratorial games;
slam our dominoes down so the table shakes.

4.
We catch ourselves in another fray;
wait each other out for hours. No way
either of us is going to give way.
'This is pointless,' you finally say,
raising a stir, troublingly real. You may
be right. Then your face begins to break
into smiles; keeps my loneliness at bay.

CHESS MOVES

After the passionate debates are over
about us doing what is right, or not,
we make our way back to the heart
or what we call the heart, but mean
as somewhere *other* within us, near
the border of where we are & where
we'd like to be –
               but just as chess moves
gain their meanings later in the game,
we come to find the heart is sometimes
missing & have to stand behind the
things we said – as one would stand
behind a poker hand, or throw of dice –
facing each other, staring at our feet;
wondering if we're rooting in the dust.

LECTURE ON THE THEORY OF BEING, NO. 33

We don't live far from our childhood
looking into light to divine the future
long before we discover the world is
full of holes – the endless night that
swallows the dream – our tongues
locating shapes & working them like thumbs.

Suddenly, all those things! & then our time
is up. Forever at that age lasts seconds.
Each moment echoes someone else's words.
The world streams on the way stalagmites
form, pointing up a sad truth time does not
erase, until we cut our tongues in the process
of speaking, like children asking how it is
possible to become younger; so eager to return.

AN OLD CARTOON

The sun unwinds itself from night's monsoon.
It is as if we've slept in separate beds
& yet I wake to the imagined smile
behind your sleeping face, tired of being
alone, or rather, welcoming the small
everyday acts that raise their heads
again & again in cheerful tones, flickering
in stop-start frames, as in an old cartoon.

It takes all day to reach the other us,
the truthful one that lies beneath the surface
of this game. Our hope lies in the scripts
we read & in our reading gathering hints
of what lights up the paper from inside;
for love's a lantern & isn't it burning bright?

LANDSCAPE WITH MOUNTAINS

Who am I? That's a good question, but
before we tackle it, please submit it
in writing, in triplicate, giving us time
to find another story – perhaps the one
about those of us who never leave home,
unless it is to search for life, guessing
which way to head. There's a story to still
the heart, for the roads it describes lead
back through years of self-satisfied comfort –
we chase the same unchanging lures
as we lumber along, searching the angles
of night & the strings of attachment, until
we find ourselves in firm defeat en route
to the mountain. The water that flows from
its peak surprises us, even though we know
it is the source. We lie enmeshed in songs
that drift down from the high meadows;
revel in the view; drink wine & eat our fill
of the exhausted sun that strides the long horizon.
There in the distance, the harbour catches
the last of the light, to the clatter of rigging.
Lovers line the seawall, blind to all but the sea.
    Now, about that question...

NO REASON
for A.S.

Now has returned from our past:
we have never been without it.
In the dim before of life's interior,
lit-up on the edge between grand theories
& elation over getting up, today is
beginning to open – a verge of soft
grass in the bright light of Spring.
For the first time in months we're
together again. On the pillow beneath
your head, spots of light & dark unite
& cancel, questioning the extent –
the *existence* – of a reason. We wake
& trace the sun with no need to be
coaxed into life: to watch you rising
from sleep will always suffice. Now is
the only season I am ever sure of being.

FRAGMENTS FOR AN INDETERMINATE FRIEND

As you approach
the air unlocks

closes behind you
as you leave.

An y other –
that y you.

*

Winter with no one
but you to talk to.

Love – the way it
stands up to silence.

*

You were a mysterious
6 foot piece of light.

*

We touched heads
our usual greeting.

Meeting you   like
crossing a mind field.

*

You drew on a cigarette
& flicked it away into grey

ragged fog. Our eyes met
across the gulf. The waves

channelled in in septets.
I couldn't look up to

the small patch of daylight
for fear of drowning.

*

Stay tonight
but leave tomorrow.

No   leave tonight
& come back tomorrow

leaving desire to balance
what may follow.

*

Our coastline was complete.
We sank in it up to our lips

shallow enough to wade across
like a wide & sluggish lagoon.

*

You sited your story elsewhere.
The *other* faded by time.

*

The driver put the wheel hard over.
I waved you off   my right hand raised

like a giant stone Buddha –
'I'm going now... goodbye...'
Alone. Rootless. Moving. Gone.
I wonder why you wanted to leave:

Wherever you go   there you are:
'Acushla... O pulse of my heart...'

*

The day ends when
you drive away.

Forgetting it has wings   night
lingers like a deserted village.

Loneliness lies scattered round
in the shade of overhanging dreams.

Sometimes   it seems
to rain up.

*

Day after day I return
with nothing but skin

always looking through
this face. Here is the clue:

picture any friendship
& see only its most recent

surface   in danger
of being loved.

PHOTO IN A MIRROR OF A WOMAN DESCENDING STAIRS

'A girl slowly descended the line of steps.'

> *— John Ashbery*

As the photograph shows it, your left hand
hovering above the handrail, the same foot
suspended in anticipation over the following
step, all seven of the spirals swerving
towards the camera & mirror, although
the staircase is behind us & we are
looking at reflections of the well,
a semblance of the steps you are descending.
The parabola of the rail neatly cuts
the image into thirds with the accuracy
of the Golden Section: a horizontal line
down one third from the frame's top edge,
another intersecting on the vertical plane,
placing your head in the perfect position
for focus. Some posters on the wall behind,
the wall itself a grey and fading stucco
& the stairs fanning out beneath your feet
almost with free will, as you hang on
step three, gazing right ahead & always
that way as the camera dictates & we
remember, each step a segment of light,
each riser black in shadow, like the dress
you are wearing, dotted with roses,
your bare legs ending in sandal'd feet,
as your image recedes in black, just the pink
of your arm & the side of your face catching
rays from the window at the stair's head,
continually throwing light between
your skin, the lens, the viewer's eyes
& into photographic memory.

Your shadow walks before you,
as though you were following the future,
leaving a French museum by a spiral
staircase — your body re-living life
as its replica — the steps' taut lines
in counterpoint to the rounded contours

of your glissade & the spiral stairs
themselves a question-mark around
anybody's bodily reality: at it's root
the certainty of dying & the lesser one
that a self-image can be built free from
the body; the illusion that what is being
shown is real, this captured process –
a descent into words – almost as if
you're climbing down on our behalf
as memory, within the film that fixes light
& fixes in us the idea that there is no
fixedness in being. So why this fixation
on bodies? No nude descending staircase
as Duchamp portrayed it previously,
but a point in space & time becoming,
which is all we can ever be sure we are
from Duchampian moment to moment;
a witness that figures are not what they
seem, but tracings – rhythmic, fluid lines
at best at peace with themselves & others.

'I had no idea you were so small!'
Picasso said apocryphally & looking at
your tiny, photogenic hands caressing
the rail (as the light caresses the eye;
the sweeping lines of steps that project
you in stillness, in light relief), it seems
entirely possible that the body's architecture
exists on such small scales: for you are neither
jogging the memory, nor stamping it in,
but treading on it lightly, here, three times
removed, with a miniature sense of potential.

DEVON APPLES
for Marcus Vergette

Spring break-up on the frozen river,
the orchard silenced except for the buzz
of insects dreaming this year's apple blossom:
"Come autumn we'll make cider, next May get drunk…"

*

Longstem's drunk with new ideas,
Blue Sweet knows they trickle down.
Hollow Core turns art into conception,
Loral Drain has purity of form.

Dufflin celebrates the new millenium,
Hoary Morning struggles with the past.
Slack Ma Girdle exploits its possibilities,
Keswick Codling isn't much impressed.

Sour Natural is coolly received by the British,
Jacob's Strawberry can't dispel the myth.
Johnny Voun redefines melody & phrasing,
Johnny Andrews' audience laughs & laughs.

*

All Doer says we're in this together,
Ben's Red was raised in the heart of the machine.
Bowden's Seedling never found a job,
Coleman's Seedling thinks the price too high.

Breadfruit have fallen out of the system,
Broomhouse Whites will fret about their debts.
Chisel Jersey trembles on the brink of revolution,
Catshead lays the consciousness to come.

Buttery d'Or witnessed a terrible beauty,
Bickington Gray saw the same thing in Europe.
Gilliflower uttered a cry of defiance,
Captain Broad sent worried letters home.

Honey Pin belongs to a circle of extremists,
Improved Pound plants stories in the patriotic press.
Quarrenden mourns glories past in empires lost,
Goring never insisted on the facts.

Early Bowers were bloodthirsty butchers,
Ellis's Bitter killed for political belief.
King Byerd admired the ancient Romans,
Golden Ball demanded the King's execution.

*

Barum met Beef when each needed the other,
Beech Bearer keeps a bottle beneath the bed.
Loyal Drong said not to bother looking,
Reynold's Peach found it just below the surface.

Sops In Wine have married & live abroad,
Crimson Victoria had second thoughts about leaving.
Woolbrook feels at home with Saw Pit,
Quoinings are ready to be themselves.

Plumderity devotes their all to Cerif,
Stockbear & Sugar Bush find they are strangers.
Queen Caroline always keeps her vigil,
The Rattler rivals her sister's best.

Plum Vite announces the evening menu,
Polly White Hair doesn't bother to dress.
No Pip pays the conjuror,
Morgan Sweet does a graceful turn.

*

Sweet Alford needs the church,
Sweet Cleave plays cards in cafés.
Pig's Nose huffs predictably,
Pig's Snout fits the mouth.

Sweet Copin enjoys a different perspective,
Tan Harvey comes into her own.
Tale Sweet announces her pregnancy,
Summer Stubbard's wish was granted.

Thin Skin exerts a mystical pull,
Tom Putt is a person of wisdom & grace.
Nine Square aggravated his heart problem,
Limberlimb was also pale.

Lucombe's Pine let small things slip,
Hangy Down tightened up on them later.
John Toucher was ready for anything,
Long Bit & Listener achieved nothing at all.

Tommy Knight clung to outdated ideas,
Tommy Potter always had the acumen.
Rawlings made final arrangements in silence,
Winter Peach died young – forgive her all.

Billy White lies in the theatre for hours,
Butterbox touches a sensitive nerve.
Oaken Pin kisses your lips,
Sidney Strake takes their final breath.

NOTES

What we Think of as Home: the poem takes its title from the poem 'Settlements' by John Burnside, beginning with the lines:

> Because what we think of as home
> is a hazard to others
> our shorelines edged with rocks and shallow
> sandbanks
> reefs
> where navigation fails

which was an inspiration for both this poem, and the littoral structuring of this collection.

The Water Cycle: 'Yes Yes' refers to the voting campaign during the run-up to the vote on an independent Scottish Assembly.

Stes-Maries-de-la-Mer: a resort of the Camargue, in Southern France. The white horses of the Camargue are semi-wild, and change colour from brown to white at around four years old. Stes-Maries has a Romanesque church, well-known for its annual Romany festival each May. Sarah was the servant of Mary Jacobé, Jesus' aunt, and Mary Salomé, mother of two of the apostles. Along with Mary Magdelene and several other New Testament characters, Sarah was driven from Palestine by the Jews, landing in a boat near the Rhône. In 1448 the relics of the women were discovered in the church, around the time the Romanies were migrating to Western Europe. Each year, the shrines and statues of the Saints are carried to the sea, and the Romanies ask for blessings from their patron saint.

Shakkei: a Japanese word translating as 'borrowed scenery'. In well-designed Japanese homes, a window frames a distant landscape feature, 'borrowing' the landscape and bringing it subtly into the house, as though in a painting.

Fragments for an Indeterminate Friend: Acushla (Gaelic): 'O pulse of my heart'.

Devon Apples: for several years I have helped my friend Marcus Vergette to make cider; from the picking of the apples, through the processes of crushing, juice extraction, fermentation, bottling and drinking. The names of the apples are all genuine varieties of Devon apple, or varieties which have a close association with the county.

ANDY BROWN is a lecturer in creative writing and arts at Exeter University. *From A Cliff* is his third collection, preceded by *The Wanderer's Prayer* (Arc, 1999), *West of Yesterday* (Stride, 1998), and two pamphlets. He co-wrote a book of poems, *Of Science* (Worple Press, 2001) with David Morley. A selection of innovative prose poems appeared in *Vital Movement: Reality Street 4Packs No. 2* (Reality Street, 1999). He set up, and runs, the Maquette Press, and is the editor of *Binary Myths: conversations with contemporary poets* (Stride, 1998), and *Binary Myths 2: correspondences with poet-editors* (Stride, 1999). A musician as well as a poet, he has performed and recorded music in the UK and USA. He now lives with his partner and two children in Exeter.